chic and simple

The last detail: 25 finishing touches

chic and simple

Andrea Spencer
Photography by Graham Rae

southwater

This edition is published by Southwater

Southwater is an imprint of
Anness Publishing Limited
Hermes House
88–89 Blackfriars Road
London SE1 8HA
tel. 020 7401 2077
fax 020 7633 9499

Distributed in the USA by
Anness Publishing Inc.
27 West 20th Street
Suite 504
New York
NY 10011
fax 212 807 6813

Distributed in the UK by
The Manning Partnership
251–253 London Road East
Batheaston
Bath BA1 7RL
tel. 01225 852 727
fax 01225 852 852

Distributed in Australia by
Sandstone Publishing
Unit 1
360 Norton Street
Leichhardt
New South Wales 2040
tel. 02 9560 7888
fax 02 9560 7488

1 3 5 7 9 10 8 6 4 2

Publisher : Joanna Lorenz
Senior Editor : Lindsay Porter
Photographer : Graham Rae
Designer : Lilian Lindblom
Stylist : Andrea Spencer

Previously published as *Interior Details*

CONTENTS

INTRODUCTION

Trimmings can completely change the look and personality of everyday objects, such as lampshades and bases, simple tablecloths and fine muslin curtains. They need not be expensive and many can be created using everyday things from around the home. Search cupboards and drawers for balls of string and lengths of twine. Don't just wrap parcels in corrugated paper – create beautiful surrounds for windows or doors and cover notebooks, candles and even straight-sided vases with it.

Take beautiful objects from nature to adorn your walls and windows. Make use of shells, pebbles and driftwood brought back from beachcombing holidays by fashioning them into pretty necklaces, glorious seaside curtains and unusual frames. Minute flower heads, seeds, berries and leaves can all be used as decoration; when giving presents, make the occasion really special by wrapping them in delicate organza and tying with a glorious bow.

Ribbons can be used to dress windows, tie up napkins or adorn lampshades for the most beautiful light show ever. It's just a matter of having the confidence and style to set to work and start creating.

As in so many things, simplicity is the key word. Take a fresh look at a skein of raffia: it could look marvellous edging shelves or tied into a tassel to hold a napkin. Likewise, a few lengths of rope can be used to dress your sofa, trim your curtains, or create a dado in the bedroom or bathroom. Where possible, use natural materials, such as cotton, linen and hessian; they have a wonderful, tactile quality and look good in any situation.

Experiment a little and gain inspiration from the ideas and projects on the following pages.

ROUND-UP WITH RIBBONS

Ribbons come in a wonderful variety of colours, textures and widths. By tying a simple loop or bow, you can give a new contrasting or complementary accent to existing furniture and furnishings. Soft, floppy, translucent organza ribbons create a cloudy frothiness when gathered in folds and bows but look simple and elegant hung against the light of a window, where they give an element of privacy and distract the eye from an unwelcome view without reducing the light at all. Rich silken ribbons, or rough linen and hessian, have completely different qualities.

Above: Often the simplest of materials are the most beautiful. Scrolls of handmade paper tied with ribbon are elegantly minimalist.

Above: Translucent ribbons used as a curtain, trimmed with dried flower heads.

Above: Dressing a lampshade with a simple organza bow, as here, creates an elegant effect. Try different ribbons to suit the style of the room.

Left: Organza ribbon on a twig and ivy wreath not only embellishes the decoration, but is also used for hanging.

TASSELS

Tassels are flourishes: they bring a jaunty, nonchalant air to the furnishings they embellish. Tassels also come in a wide variety of materials and colours. The simplest can be home-made from household materials such as string, which is perfectly in keeping with decorated old terracotta pots. Made from natural materials, they bring a touch of style to design schemes based on neutral colours and natural fabrics; in rich colours and silken threads they are opulent or restrained, depending on how they are combined. Rich red combined with a natural linen table napkin is a sunburst of bright colour that lifts, but doesn't disrupt, the neutral scheme. A traditional white tassel combined with a brick red throw quilted in a simple, modern style is a graphic and contemporary interpretation of a classic upholsterery trimming.

Above: The simplicity of the plain muslin curtain and bamboo poles has been complemented by the natural tassel. The effect is understated yet eye-catching.

Above: Decorated plant pots are enhanced by a home-made string tassel.

Above: Brightly coloured tassels make the simplest and most chic napkin rings. Choose colours that complement your china — they could be matching or vividly contrasting.

Left: An upholstery tassel gives a sophisticated finish to the corner of a throw.

ON THE CARDS

Home-made cards go beyond mere stationery, and can become miniature works of art in their own right. Use to grace a mantelpiece or occasional table. You can base them on bought plain card blanks or search for wonderful textured paper and cardboard to make your own. Then collect pressed leaves, flower heads and other natural materials, and combine these with contemporary details such as gold paint and writing and organza ribbon. For a perfectly simple, contemporary interpretation, take the plainest white card and embellish it with a graceful paper curl – minimalism at its best.

Above: A contemporary white card simply adorned with an orange paper curl creates a striking effect.

Right: This plain gold card is beautifully decorated with an oak leaf and ribbon.

Opposite: Decorating plain handmade paper with natural materials produces true works of art.

TURNING THE CORNER

The corners and edges of cushions are a good opportunity for embellishments, especially when, as here, the cushion-cover fabric itself is plain. All of these details maintain and enhance the style of the cushions, which are made from natural materials in a range of neutral colours, as are the trimmings themselves. This shows how you can make detailed decorations with traditional sewing and embroidery techniques but interpret them in contemporary materials. The result is fully in keeping with today's fashion for interior-design schemes based on natural materials.

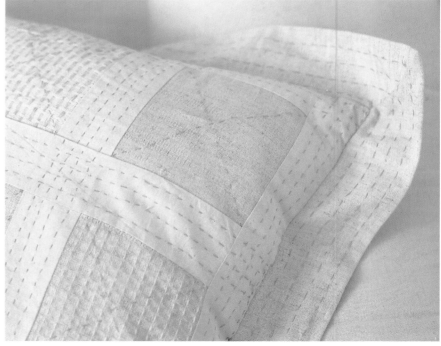

Above: White cords are simply sewn to an off-white, rough linen cushion, with graceful loops at the corners.

Above: Running-stitch "quilting" creates a neutral-on-neutral interpretation for a cushion.

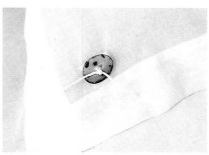

Left: A "tortoiseshell" button and string trim on snowy-white linen provides an elegant finish using the simplest of materials and techniques.

Above: Edge a cushion with toning beads on natural twine. Contrasting buttons can be used as accents of colour, picking up the shades in the rest of the decor.

STICKS AND STONES

Treasures from nature are the perfect embellishments for decoration schemes based on natural fabrics and colours. Needing no craft or art to give them charm, natural objects have their own intrinsic beauty of form, texture and colour. You may well have souvenirs of beachcombing, mountain walks, strolls though autumnal woods or spring fields that you would like to preserve; once you have the idea, every trip out of doors becomes a potential treasure-hunting expedition, if you just keep your eyes and your mind open. Collections of shells, stones, leaves and driftwood can be assembled as decorative focal points that can be rearranged or reassembled elsewhere in a moment. Alternatively, give your treasures a more permanent home by incorporating them into furnishings and accessories.

Above: A shell collection on a window ledge makes a beautiful display with translucent shells glowing when the sun shines through them.

Righ: Shells can be used as unusual candle-holders, but make sure the bases are stable.

Above: This vase is adorned with coloured stones and pieces of glass worn smooth by the action of the waves. Use as many or as few as you wish to create the finish you desire.

Right: Wicker slippers are embellished with the tiniest of starfish.

SHELL SHOCKED

Wandering along the seashore collecting

shells is a wonderfully therapeutic

pastime. After holidaying, rather than

simply keeping a selection of shells on the

sill, make them into something really

special. We have used lengths of fine voile

for curtains and added interest to the

heading by making eyelets along the top

and threading them with string loops.

To continue the theme, a really easy, yet

effective, way of trimming a wall is to use

a length of fine rope (available from DIY

stores or yacht chandlers). Attach this to

the wall at dado height; it would also

look extremely effective at picture-rail

height. Fix a row of tiny shells above.

To complete the light, airy feel, paint an

old terracotta pot white and attach a small

sand dollar or other shell to the front.

YOU WILL NEED

- ◆ iron-on interfacing (if required)
- ◆ tape measure
- ◆ dressmaker's scissors
- ◆ cotton voile, the required drop, and 4 x the window width
- ◆ dressmaker's pins
- ◆ needle and tacking thread
- ◆ sewing machine
- ◆ matching sewing thread
- ◆ chrome eyelets
- ◆ hammer
- ◆ wooden block
- ◆ rough natural string
- ◆ glue gun and glue sticks
- ◆ electric drill, with very fine drill bit (optional)
- ◆ fine beading wire
- ◆ beading needle (optional)
- ◆ terracotta pot
- ◆ matt white emulsion paint
- ◆ paintbrush
- ◆ sand dollar shell

1 To give extra body to the headings of fine fabrics, cut a length of iron-on interfacing 5 cm/2 in wide and bond it to the wrong side of the voile.

2 Pin, tack, press and machine-stitch the heading across the top and the hem at the bottom. Then turn under a 1cm/½ in hem down each side, pin, tack, press and sew.

3 Mark the positions of the eyelets with pins.

5 Cut equal lengths of string to tie through the eyelets.

7 Cut lengths of wire and use a glue gun to stick them on to the shells.

4 Fix the eyelets, following the manufacturer's instructions. Make sure you find a secure surface when hammering the eyelets in place, such as a wooden block. One short, sharp blow with the hammer should do the trick.

6 Thread the strings through the eyelets and knot the ends.

8 Alternatively, drill holes in the shells. You might find a combination of these methods helpful, depending on the shape of the shells.

9 Position the shells on the curtains.

11 Paint the flowerpot white.

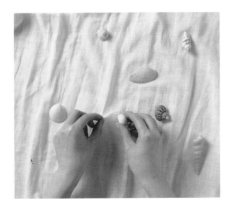

10 "Sew" the shells on to the curtain by hand, as invisibly as possible, with the beading wire.

12 Put a little glue on the side of the pot and attach the sand dollar.

Top and above: Even as light filters through the muslin, the wire fixings in the shells remain invisible.

Opposite: The voile curtains are threaded on a bamboo pole, which is totally in keeping with the natural feel of the decoration. Part of the charm is that the pole is slightly crooked.

LEADING LIGHTS

Strike a light! Change your shade and lamp base within the space of an hour to something quite sensational. Here, a basic shade was decorated with rough string threaded through punched holes. It is very easy to punch holes around the top and base of any shade, using a hole punch, and then thread through raffia, ribbon or wool. To continue this idea, put small string bows at intervals around the shade and intersperse them with dried leaves.

YOU WILL NEED

- lamp base and shade
- hole punch
- rough string
- scissors
- glue gun and glue sticks
- dried leaves

1 Punch evenly spaced holes around the top and bottom of the shade. Oversew lengths of string through the holes, top and bottom.

2 Use the glue gun to stick the leaves around the shade.

3 Tie small string bows and glue them between the leaves.

4 Put a line of glue down the back of the metal base. Starting from the top, bind a long length of string tightly around the stem. Use a second length of string to cover the base. Press to make sure the string binding is absolutely firm. Make sure that the ends are glued securely in place.

LIFE'S LITTLE LUXURIES

Cushions are the perfect way to add a certain style to your room, as well as an element of comfort. Here, the choice of natural tones and fabrics perfectly complement the simplicity of the sofa. Interest was added to the restrained look with decorative ties, looped buttons and a simple rope trim. If you want a change from the neutral colour scheme shown here, add splashes of vibrant colour with blues, reds, oranges and purples. Alternatively, blue and white always looks fresh and pretty.

YOU WILL NEED

ROPE-TRIMMED CUSHION

- about 2m / 2yd fine-gauge rope
- dressmaker's pins
- plain linen cushion cover
- needle and matching sewing thread
- cushion pad

CUSHION WITH TIES

- cushion pad
- tape measure
- cotton duck
- dressmaker's scissors
- dressmaker's pins
- needle and tacking thread
- sewing machine
- matching sewing thread

LOOP AND BUTTON CUSHION

- cushion pad
- 1m/1yd linen
- dressmaker's scissors
- dressmaker's pins
- needle and tacking thread
- sewing machine
- matching sewing thread
- iron
- 8–10 small buttons

1 For the rope-trimmed cushion cover, use the fine-gauge rope to experiment with different designs. When you are happy with the result, pin the rope on to the cover.

2 Hand-stitch the cord to the cover, neatly finishing off the ends. Insert the cushion pad.

3 For the cushion with ties, measure the cushion pad and cut one piece of fabric the depth of the cushion plus 1.5cm/⅝ in all round for seams. Cut another piece to twice the length, plus an extra 16.5cm/6½ in for the turning (this allows 1.5cm/⅝ in for a hem also). Pin, tack, press and sew, taking in the seam allowance.

5 For the ties, cut six pieces of fabric measuring 6 x 28cm/2¼ x 11in.

7 Position the ties in pairs and pin and tack them in place. Then topstitch them securely in position.

4 Trim and zigzag stitch the raw edges together, to neaten them. Turn the cushion right-side out.

6 Fold each piece in half lengthways with wrong sides together and pin, tack, press and machine-stitch a 1cm/½in hem round two sides. Clip the seams and corners. Turn the ties right sides out and slip-stitch the ends closed.

8 For the cushion with loops and buttons, measure the width and length of the cushion pad. Double the length and add 10cm/4in for the flap opening, plus 3cm/1¼in for seams all around. You will also need to cut a 7.5cm/3in wide strip, the depth of the cushion plus seams. Cut fabric to this size and fold it in half.

9 To make the piping for the button loops cut a length of fabric about 2.5cm/1in wide, on the cross. With wrong sides together, pin, tack and machine-stitch the fabric. Trim close to the stitching and, using a small safety pin, turn through to the right side. Press flat.

11 Pin, tack and sew the interfacing strip for the back opening on the edge with the loops.

10 Measure the buttons and cut the loops to the correct size. Turn over the seam allowance on the cover, then pin and tack the loops in place.

12 With right sides together, sew a seam all around the cushion. Turn right-side out and press. Mark the positions of the buttons with pins, and sew in place.

Right: These cushions complement the simplicity of the decor. Interest is added with flamboyant ties and other trimmings.

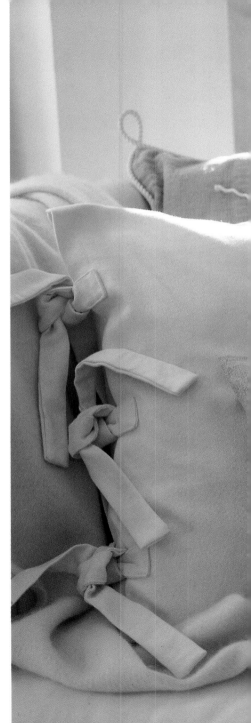

IT'S A WRAP

When decorating a table for a very special occasion, go to town and trim accordingly. These ideas could not be simpler to achieve, but will add to the festive spirit.

YOU WILL NEED

♦ teapot

♦ scissors

♦ about 10cm/4in square organza, net or other fine fabric

♦ pot-pourri

♦ very fine string

♦ small cinnamon stick

♦ glue gun and glue sticks

♦ glass bottle

♦ star anises

♦ decanter

♦ organza ribbon

♦ 2 heart-shaped silver beads

♦ fresh rose

♦ painted jar

♦ florist's wire

♦ small fresh flower sprigs

1 For the teapot decoration, cut a circle from the organza and fill it with pot-pourri. Tie the top with string. Twist a cinnamon stick into the tie. To finish, tie the bag to the knob of the teapot.

2 To make the bottle necklace, cut a piece of fine string, and pull apart to separate the strands. Glue star anises to one strand. Knot the ends and hang it on the bottle.

3 To decorate the decanter, take a piece of organza ribbon and thread the heart-shaped bead on to it. Knot it around the neck of the decanter and tie in a fresh rose head.

4 To decorate the painted jar, tie a very fine piece of string around the neck. Wire two or three strands of flowers together and secure them under the string. Tie an organza bow around the knob of the lid.

THE NEW WAVE

Corrugated paper is a much-maligned material that can look absolutely stunning if used innovatively. It is easy to work with and has myriad uses. Experiment with different shapes to see which looks most pleasing. Triangles would look great bordering a door frame, for example, and perhaps following the lines of the skirting.

Bear in mind that corrugated paper crushes very easily so, before starting work, flatten it with a ruler. It will still look ridged but won't mark. A lovely idea is to paint corrugated paper white and then slit the corrugations, giving a two-tone effect. Coloured corrugated paper is available from art shops.

YOU WILL NEED

- ◆ tape measure
- ◆ roll of natural corrugated paper
- ◆ scissors
- ◆ ruler
- ◆ thin cardboard
- ◆ pencil
- ◆ craft knife
- ◆ self-healing cutting mat
- ◆ aerosol adhesive
- ◆ masking tape (optional)
- ◆ candles
- ◆ white emulsion paint
- ◆ paintbrush
- ◆ glue gun and glue sticks
- ◆ natural string
- ◆ straight-sided vase
- ◆ fine corrugated paper in different colours
- ◆ paper glue

1 Measure the width of the sill and cut the corrugated paper to this measurement, plus the required drop. Flatten the ridges with a ruler.

2 Draw the design on to cardboard and cut out to use as a template.

3 Draw the shape on the natural corrugated paper, using the template. Cut it out with a craft knife on a cutting mat.

5 For the candle-wrappers, cut strips of corrugated paper to the right size and paint them with white emulsion. Slit the corrugations with scissors.

7 To make the picture frame, measure the image that will be framed and decide on the size and shape required.

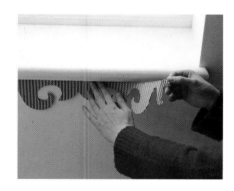

4 Spray the back of the corrugated paper with aerosol adhesive and fix in position. If you want to remove the decoration later, stick masking tape under the windowsill and glue the decoration to the tape. You can peel off the tape without harming the wall.

6 Cut a wider strip and glue it to the back of the white strip. Wrap the decoration round the candles. Cut string long enough to wrap several times round the candles. Use the same technique to make a decoration for a straight-sided vase.

8 Draw the frame backing on to corrugated cardboard and cut it out with the craft knife and ruler.

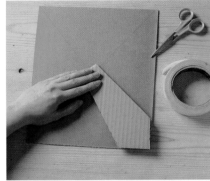

9 Use the backing as a template to draw and cut out the front of the frame from coloured corrugated paper. Cut out the central frame area.

11 Make a stand for the frame, with a piece of corrugated cardboard cut to the shape shown. Decorate the frame with twisted strips of coloured paper.

10 Stick the image in position with paper glue so the backing colour shows through in a thin border all round.

Right: Use corrugated cardboard and paper to make borders for windows and doors. You can complete the look with decorative holders for candles, picture frames and book covers.

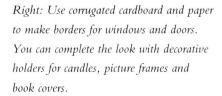

HANGING AROUND

Make the prettiest of chandelier-hangings with simple twigs such as apple or pear branches. Select a few branches and bind them together to make a pleasing shape, then hang the decoration in the centre of a window, from a ceiling rose in a hallway or as a wall decoration. Trim the branches with crystal droplets, tiny pearls, and other decorative items, all fixed with the finest of gold twine.

YOU WILL NEED

- ◆ 2–3 apple or pear tree branches
- ◆ fine gold wire
- ◆ scissors
- ◆ 1m/1yd gold cord
- ◆ crystal droplets
- ◆ gold beading wire
- ◆ small pearls
- ◆ gilded decorations

1 Take the branches and move them around until they form a pretty shape. Bind the branches together at the top with fine gold wire.

2 Attach a length of gold cord to hang the branches

3 Thread crystal droplets on to gold wire. Make short strings of pearls. If you like, combine some of the pearls with crystals.

4 Wire the remaining decorations, then twist the wires to make hanging loops. Hang the twig chandelier in position in preparation for decorating, and then hang on the jewels.

SEASIDE SETTING

Soothe the soul by strolling along the sea-shore and at the same time, scour the beach for wonderful finds: strands of seaweed, pieces of driftwood, soft grey pebbles, birds' feathers and chalky white stones with holes ready-made for threading them on to pieces of twine. Make the most of your natural treasures by using them to decorate mirrors and picture frames, or any other plain objects – their uses are endless. Sea shells make wonderfully evocative candle holders, and can be used as part of the table setting for a sea-themed dinner or party.

YOU WILL NEED

DRIFTWOOD AND PEBBLE FRAMES
- ◆ distressed-wood frames
- ◆ PVA glue (optional)
- ◆ medium-grade sandpaper
- ◆ wood stain and paintbrush (optional)
- ◆ about 50cm/20in thick rope
- ◆ staple gun or hammer and tacks
- ◆ driftwood
- ◆ glue gun and glue sticks
- ◆ seaweed
- ◆ pebbles and stones
- ◆ sea shells

PEBBLE AND STONE NECKLACES
- ◆ raffia
- ◆ tiny pebbles
- ◆ smooth coloured glass
- ◆ glue gun and glue sticks

SHELL CANDLEHOLDERS
- ◆ burnt-down candles
- ◆ kitchen knife
- ◆ sea shells
- ◆ safety matches

1 For the driftwood frame, first check that the frame is sturdy and re-glue the joints, if necessary.

2 Sand the frame along the grain and stain it, if you like.

3 To hang the mirror, attach the rope to the top of the frame, using a staple gun or hammer and tacks.

5 Use a glue gun to fix the driftwood in place, making sure the pieces are perfectly secure.

7 When you are happy with your design, glue the pebbles and other materials in place.

4 Arrange your pieces of driftwood around the frame. Experiment with different positions until you are happy with the result.

6 Work out the position of the seaweed so it drapes gently across the mirror. Add the pebbles, stones and shells, raising them slightly off the edge so they are reflected into the mirror.

8 For the pebble frame, use a similar frame base to the driftwood frame and sand and stain as before, if required. Select a pleasing variety of stones and arrange and glue them on the frame.

9 For the pebble and stone necklace, tie a length of raffia around tiny stones and pieces of smooth coloured glass.

11 For the candles in shells, cut the candles right down with a knife and stand them in a shell. Light the candles and allow the wax to drip down until it fills the shell. Blow out the flame. The wax then solidifies to the shape of the shell.

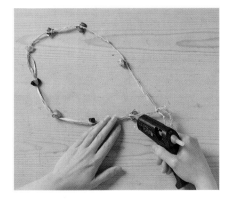

10 Use a glue gun to apply a tiny dot of glue to each knot where the stone or glass is tied.

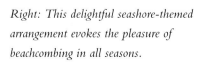

Right: This delightful seashore-themed arrangement evokes the pleasure of beachcombing in all seasons.

SELF CONTAINED

There is a variety of boxes available, ranging from simple white wooden boxes through to shoe boxes. Make a set of three using natural materials. Boxes can be trimmed with anything: bottle tops, paper clips, string, rope or a collage of stamps. Linen tape (used in upholstery or for tags) is available from haberdashery departments.

YOU WILL NEED

♦ plain wooden box

♦ tape measure

♦ scissors

♦ linen tape

♦ needle and matching sewing thread

♦ 2 wooden beads or toggles

♦ glue gun and glue sticks

♦ larch twig

♦ small slatted wooden box

♦ small packet of pot-pourri

♦ small Shaker-style box

♦ dried leaves and fir cones

1 Measure the plain wooden box. Allow an extra 2cm/¾in at one end for the toggle and about 7.5cm/3in for the loop and tag. Cut two lengths of linen tape to this length. Sew a loop in the end of each tape and attach the beads to be used as toggles.

2 Secure the tape to one end of the box with glue, leaving the toggle and loop free so the lid can be opened. Repeat on the other side. Glue a larch twig to the top of the lid, as a decorative "handle".

3 For the slatted wooden box, sort through the pot-pourri and choose the items you would like to use. Glue them to the lid. Glue the dried leaves and cones to the Shaker box, and glue linen tape around the sides.

COPYCATS

Create a truly beautiful setting by mixing fine, snowy-white linens, soft, filmy voile and crunchy tissue paper with dashes of gold in lettering and initials. It is extremely impressive to look at and, although quite time-consuming, easy to execute. Take any pieces of script or calligraphy that especially appeal to you (here, the frontispiece from some sheet music was used). Photocopy and enlarge the sections you like and trace through the photocopies on to the voile, linen and tissue paper. This process could be repeated on walls, furniture, picture frames and so on. When giving someone a present, copy a few letters in gold on to tissue or tracing paper and tie the gift with fine organza ribbon.

YOU WILL NEED
- printed calligraphy such as sheet music, old letter, wrapping paper, or the template provided in the back of the book
- voile for curtain
- masking tape
- gold fabric paint
- fine paintbrushes
- iron
- tissue paper
- gold acrylic paint
- organza ribbon
- linen hand towel
- carbon paper or soft pencil (optional)
- hard pencil (optional)

2 Photocopy the scripts or template, if using, enlarging them to size. Experiment by moving the pieces of script around to create pleasing combinations and arrangements.

1 Select your chosen examples of script. You may not find everything you need from one source, so look out for individual details.

3 Position the photocopies on the voile for the curtain, devising a pattern along its length.

4 Tape your photocopy to a table or work surface, ensuring it is flat and free of wrinkles.

6 Using gold fabric paint and a fine paintbrush, carefully trace the lettering from the photocopy on to the voile.

8 For the wrapping paper, trace different types of writing on to tissue paper, using gold acrylic paint.

5 Tape the fabric on top, so you can see the script through it clearly.

7 Press the fabric following the manufacturers' instructions, to set the colour.

9 Complement the wrapping paper with a bow of organza ribbon.

10 For the monogrammed hand towel, use paper cut-outs to plan your design.

12 Lay the towel over the alphabet, and tape flat.

14 If you wish to apply an initial to a chair or other piece of furniture, put carbon paper on to the back of the photocopied lettering, or rub all over the back with a soft pencil. Then transfer this to the furniture, by going over the outline with a harder pencil. Paint over the outline and leave to dry.

11 Tape the chosen letter flat on to a work surface.

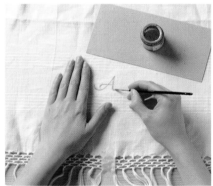

13 Trace over the letter on to the towel with the fabric paint.

Opposite: Gold calligraphy on the sheerest of materials adds elegance to a corner of a room. Look out for mottoes or phrases appropriate to the location.

NEW WAYS WITH NAPKINS

Napkins in jewel-bright colours add a wonderful splash of brilliance to any table and immediately conjure up visions of hotter climes and exotic places. Choose wools in strong colours to edge the napkins and trim each one in a different style, adding buttons and beads where appropriate.

YOU WILL NEED

- ◆ coloured linen napkins
- ◆ coloured tapestry wools
- ◆ tapestry needle
- ◆ large button
- ◆ about 50 tiny multicoloured beads
- ◆ tailor's chalk (optional)

1 If your napkin has an open-work edging, work cross-stitch following the decorative holes in the edge. If not, work evenly spaced cross-stitch along the edge. Attach a button with tapestry wool at one corner.

2 Work the edge of the second napkin with blanket stitch (see Techniques). To make the tie, take a few strands of tapestry wool, knot them in the centre and stitch them to one corner.

3 For the bead edging, work out a design by arranging the beads on a flat surface. You could mark these on the napkin first, by chalking tiny dots where you feel the beads should be. Sew the beads securely. in place.

4 Complete the edging with running stitch. Simply take the thread and weave it in and out of the fabric at regular intervals, to form a pretty line of stitches about 1cm/½in from the edge.

THROUGH A GLASS SPARKLY

The plainest of glasses and decanters can look extra special when dressed with delicate strands of gold, diamanté and jewel-coloured stones. For a party when you want to create a splash for one evening, these can be temporary arrangements, using masking tape sprayed gold and arranged in different patterns. The tape can be peeled or washed off after use. If you are prepared to spend a little longer, paint the glasses and glue stones on for good.

YOU WILL NEED

- ◆ masking tape
- ◆ self-healing cutting mat or cardboard
- ◆ gold aerosol paint
- ◆ scalpel
- ◆ metal ruler
- ◆ various glasses
- ◆ flat-backed diamanté jewels
- ◆ glue gun and glue sticks or other adhesive
- ◆ burnt match
- ◆ tweezers
- ◆ gold or silver beading wire
- ◆ decorative beads
- ◆ dried leaves
- ◆ gold ribbon

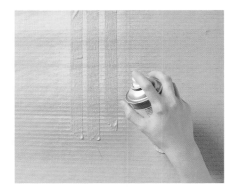

2 Spray the tape with gold aerosol paint, and leave to dry.

3 Using the scalpel and metal ruler, cut the tape into fine lengths about 5mm / ¼in wide.

1 Lay strips of masking tape across the cutting mat or cardboard.

4 Apply the strips to the bowls of the glasses, keeping clear of the rim.

5 To stick diamanté jewels to the glasses, use a glue gun and glue sticks, or use a burnt match to apply small spots of your chosen adhesive.

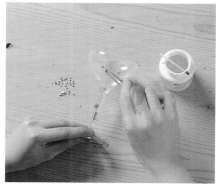

6 Stick the jewels directly to the glass, positioning them with a pair of tweezers.

7 Attach beading wire by winding a long length round the top of a glass. Criss-cross the wire down the glass.

8 Thread a decorative bead on to the wire half-way up the stem. Secure in place with a dab of glue.

9 Alternatively, twine wire around the stem, binding it round and round quite loosely.

11 Again, thread a decorative bead on to the wire half-way up the stem. You can create all kinds of variations on this theme to make a set of glasses.

12 Dress the stems of glasses with leaves, sprayed gold or silver. Attach them by slotting them into a ribbon around the stem of the glass.

Right: Turn plain glasses into festive and opulent vessels with gold and diamanté jewel decorations for a truly baroque-style special occasion. The effect can be created temporarily or permanently.

CURTAIN CALL

This is an extremely quick and effective way to trim the top edge of a loop-headed curtain. Tie ribbons round the loops and hang a selection of beautiful decorations from them. Here we have used pieces of pot- pourri but you could also use odd earrings, bells, tin stars, buttons and so on. If you have a pinch-pleated or a simple gathered curtain heading, a small bow or knot with ribbon hanging down would look effective.

YOU WILL NEED
- ◆ **tape measure**
- ◆ **1cm/½in wide hessian or linen ribbon or tape**
- ◆ **dressmaker's scissors**
- ◆ **needle and matching sewing thread (optional)**
- ◆ **pot-pourri**
- ◆ **glue gun and glue sticks**

1 Decide the length of ribbon or tape needed in relation to the drop of the curtain, so that it looks in proportion.

2 Cut the ribbon or tape to length and cut the ends at an angle, so they look neat. If you are using a ribbon that frays, hem the ends. Select the pieces of pot-pourri that most complement one another.

3 Using a glue gun, attach the pieces of pot-pourri to the ends of the ribbon or tape.

4 Tie the ribbon or tape to the curtain loops. It is best not to fix them permanently, so you can change the design when you wish and take them off when you wash the curtains.

LOVELY LINENS

Pretty up perfectly plain linens with splashes of vibrant colour. To add definition, run strips of rick-rack edging around; for frilliness, buy broderie anglaise and sew this on to the pillowcase. You could weave tapestry wool through the broderie in place of ribbon, to add colour. Alternatively, look for linens which have a fine-holed edging and thread through this with fine tapestry wool. To complement the edges, add tiny crosses of coloured thread to buttons sewn on to the pillowcase. A more time-consuming but extremely effective deocoration is made by scalloping the edge of a sheet.

YOU WILL NEED

- ♦ paper
- ♦ pencil
- ♦ cardboard
- ♦ scissors
- ♦ single or double white sheet
- ♦ sewing machine
- ♦ white sewing thread
- ♦ small, sharp-pointed scissors
- ♦ red tapestry wool
- ♦ tapestry needle
- ♦ plain pillowcase
- ♦ 3m/3yd broderie anglaise
- ♦ dressmaker's pins
- ♦ needle and tacking thread
- ♦ buttoned pillowcase, with fine-holed decorative edge
- ♦ glue gun and glue sticks
- ♦ decorative red buttons
- ♦ small cushion, with frilled-edge and centre-opening cover

1 Try various design options for the shape of the scalloped edge of the sheet, or trace the template from the back of the book, enlarging if required.

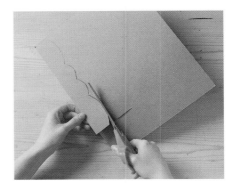

2 Transfer your chosen design to cardboard and cut out the template for the sheet edging.

3 Put the template on the edge of the sheet and draw round it all along the edge. Use machine satin-stitch to go over the outline, using the closest stitch possible. Very carefully cut along the sewing line, close to the sewing but taking care not to snip any stitches. Cut lengths of tapestry wool and knot the ends.

5 Edge the plain pillowcase with broderie anglaise, pinning and tacking it in place. Machine-stitch it securely.

7 For the buttoned pillowcase, make neat cross-stitches over the buttons with tapestry wool.

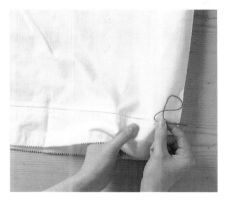

6 Using a tapestry needle, thread the tapestry wool through the holes in the broderie anglaise.

8 Thread tapestry wool through the fine-holed decorative edge.

4 Sew the lengths of tapestry wool through the sheet, leaving the long ends to form a decorative edge.

9 Use a glue gun to apply decorative red buttons on to existing buttons on the frilled–edged cushion cover.

Right: A whole variety of ideas for bed linen and cushions is shown here, all using a red and white theme that would be perfect for warming up a neutral colour scheme.

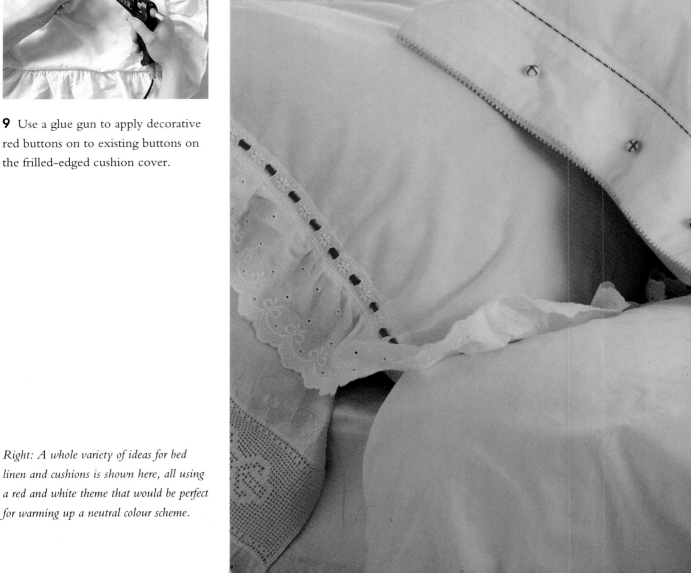

FABULOUS FURNITURE

Trim a perfectly plain sofa with a strand of rope that curves gently down the edge of the arm and across the base. This works extremely well in a white-on-white scheme, because the eye is aware of the shape but the embellishment doesn't jump out. Other types of trimming for sofas could be raffia edging, linen tassels or fringing.

YOU WILL NEED

- ◆ graph or plain paper
- ◆ pencil
- ◆ rope, the length of the area you wish to trim
- ◆ clear sticky tape
- ◆ scissors
- ◆ dressmaker's pins
- ◆ needle and strong sewing thread

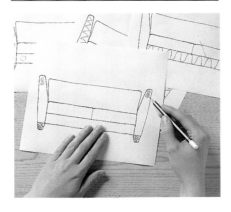

1 Work out different designs for the rope on paper, to see what works the best; this style seemed sympathetic to the shape of the arm of the sofa and the lines of the seat.

2 Bind clear sticky tape around the ends of the rope, so that the ends don't fray once the rope is in position.

3 Cut as close to the end of the tape as you can, so that as little is left as possible, but it still holds the rope firmly. Pin the rope on to the sofa and hand-stitch in place.

UNDER COVER

A seat cover in a yellow check is a lovely way to trim a chair and hide an ugly seat. Chair covers bring instant colour and style to a room; using yellow checks and stripes immediately brings to mind buttercups, marigolds and the countryside. A pretty frill around the edge finishes off this seat cover, giving the chair great femininity and charm.

YOU WILL NEED

- ♦ tape measure
- ♦ paper, for template
- ♦ pencil
- ♦ scissors
- ♦ fabric (see step 1 to calculate the amount)
- ♦ dressmaker's scissors
- ♦ piping cord
- ♦ needle and tacking thread
- ♦ sewing machine with zipper foot
- ♦ matching sewing thread
- ♦ iron
- ♦ about 1m/1yd tape

1 Make a paper template of the chair seat. Use the template as a guide to cut out the fabric with a 1.5cm/⅝ in seam allowance all round. For the frill, cut a piece twice the circumference of the seat with a 10cm/4in drop, plus a 1.5cm/⅝ in seam allowance all round.

2 Cut a length of piping cord and a 2.5cm/1in strip of fabric the length of the four sides of the chair seat. Fold the fabric around the cord, with wrong sides together. Pin, tack and stitch.

3 Hem the frill. Sew a line of running stitches around the top of the frill and then gather it up evenly.

4 Sandwich the piping cord between the frill and the seat cover, right-sides together. The piping and frill will extend around the front and sides of the seat cover. Pin, tack, press and machine-stitch all round, clipping the corners so the frill sits properly. Attach lengths of tape to the back of the seat cover, to tie the cover in position.

CREAM TOPPING

Make a grand statement at the window by creating a pelmet with a curved edge trimmed with rope. The gentle wave of the pelmet gives a very gracious, elegant appearance to the treatment, which could, if you wish, be echoed in the edging of a loose cover on a chair or sofa. Another wonderful idea is to continue the pelmet right around the room, so it acts as a wavy trim to the whole area. In this instance, make sure the pelmet is the same colour as the ceiling so it doesn't interrupt the eye's progress. Pelmets can be any shape or size; experiment with pointed V's with bells on, castellations and the like. Cut the shape out of paper first and pin it above the curtains to see what effect it will have upon the window and the room as a whole.

YOU WILL NEED

- ◆ tape measure
- ◆ paper, for template
- ◆ 2 plates
- ◆ pencil
- ◆ pelmet fabric
- ◆ dressmaker's scissors
- ◆ interfacing
- ◆ dressmaker's pins
- ◆ needle and tacking thread
- ◆ sewing machine
- ◆ matching sewing thread
- ◆ iron
- ◆ rope
- ◆ wooden batten
- ◆ hammer and tacks or Velcro

1 Measure the window and decide on the dimensions of the pelmet. Allow an extra 5cm/2in to fix to the batten. Use the plates to make a template.

2 Cut two pieces of fabric for the back and the front of the pelmet. Cut out interfacing to stiffen the pelmet, and pin the three layers, together, with right sides facing.

3 Draw round the template on to the pelmet piece with a pencil.

4 Pin the fabric just inside the scalloped outline.

6 Tack along the edge, then machine-stitch with matching sewing thread.

8 Turn the pelmet right-side out and press the scalloped edge.

5 Cut out the scallops about 1cm/½in from the outline.

7 Trim the interfacing and clip the seam allowance so that the curves will lie flat when turned right-side out.

9 Turn under the straight edge of the pelmet, then pin and machine-stitch.

10 Measure the scalloped edge and cut a length of rope to fit. Experiment with design options for the rope; for example, you could use two different colours and weights of rope.

11 Pin the rope to the pelmet and hand-sew it in place. To attach the pelmet to the wall, use a slim batten of wood and nail the pelmet to it; or use Velcro to make the pelmet easy to remove.

Above: The neutral colours used gives the gentle shape of the pelmet a chance to make an understated impact.

Opposite: The natural linen curtains echo the pelmet fabric and are lined in a slightly darker linen, so they even look beautiful when turned back upon themselves.

SHELL TIE-BACK

Curtain tie-backs can be made in a tremendously wide range of styles so you can use them to create whatever decorative effect you like. Though we normally think of a simple braid or tassel, tie-backs can be trimmed to make them focal- and talking-points within the room. Here a fishing net was festooned with different types and sizes of shells. You could wire a mass of very small shells on to the net or edge the curtain with a widely spaced line of shells.

YOU WILL NEED

- ♦ fishing net
- ♦ shells
- ♦ fine wire
- ♦ wire cutters
- ♦ glue gun and glue sticks or electric drill, with very fine drill bit
- ♦ string (optional)

2 Alternatively, drill holes in the shells. Thread string through the holes, for attaching to the net.

1 Take the fishing net and arrange it in graceful folds. Gather together a mass of shells and see how they look best when arranged on the net. Cut lengths of fine wire. These can be glued to the back of the shells so that they can be wired on to the netting.

3 Fix the shells on the netting. Make another tie-back in the same way Loop the tie-backs around the curtains and on to the wall.

CRYSTAL TIE-BACK

Mix an exquisite striped silk with crystal

drops for an elegant tie-back. The trim

made from a very rough hessian, bound

quite casually and loosely, makes this

interesting and unusual. The crystal drops

were bought from an antique shop; search

around for interesting examples. Failing

that, use crystal drops from a bead shop

or coloured stones from a cheap necklace

or earrings, all of which will look

equally lovely.

YOU WILL NEED

- ◆ 1 hessian tassel tie-back
- ◆ scissors
- ◆ crystal chandelier drops
- ◆ gold beading wire or very fine gold string
- ◆ wire cutters

1 You only need one tassel tie-back for two curtains. Split the tassel in half, then unravel the rope. Re-bind the tassel to make it look less formal.

2 Thread the crystal drops on to gold wire or fine string to make several lengths of various sizes.

3 Fasten the lengths of crystal drops on to the tie-backs. Some will simply hook on; others should be wired. Loop the tie-backs around the curtains and on to the wall.

SHEER MAGIC

Trim a plain linen or hessian bed cover and pillowcase with the sheerest of voile fabrics, to give a look which is simple, tailored and very elegant. Large bone buttons and the rougher textures of hessian and linen are the perfect foil to the fineness of the fabric. Cut the voile a tiny bit longer than the drop on the bed so it falls gently on to the floor all the way round. The voile cover is cut in three pieces, so it is easily removed and can be washed and dried within a matter of hours. The amount of voile fabric given here is for a double bed, but the basic idea can be adapted to suit any size bed.

YOU WILL NEED

- ◆ tape measure
- ◆ about 7m/7yd cotton voile
- ◆ dressmaker's scissors
- ◆ dressmaker's pins
- ◆ needle and tacking thread
- ◆ sewing machine
- ◆ matching sewing thread
- ◆ hessian or fine linen bed cover
- ◆ 16 large bone buttons
- ◆ fine embroidery scissors
- ◆ tapestry needle
- ◆ fine string
- ◆ pillow
- ◆ hessian or fine linen

1 For the top of the cover, you will need a piece of voile the length of the bed plus the drop on one end. The piece should be 15cm/6in narrower than the width of the bed so the buttons will not be too near the edge. Allow 10cm/4in all round for double hems. For the sides, you will need two pieces the length of the bed. Measure the drop from the buttons to the floor, allowing hems as before.

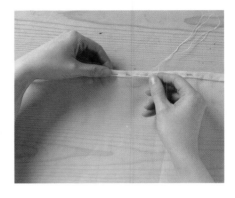

2 Pin, tack and sew all the hems.

3 Mark the positions of the buttons and buttonholes so they correspond exactly. Sew the buttonholes and cut the centres carefully.

4 Use a tapestry needle to thread fine string through the buttons. Tie the string in a knot. Sew the buttons in position on the hessian bed cover, and button the voile cover on top.

6 With right sides together, pin, tack and sew the top and bottom edges. Turn right-side out and press.

8 Use the same method to make an over-cover for the pillow from voile. Hem all the edges.

5 For the pillowcase, cut a piece of hessian the depth of the pillow and twice the length, plus seam allowances on the long sides.

7 To make a fringed edge, find a thread running across the pillow, just in from the cut edge. Pull gently to fray the edge.

9 Mark the position of the button-holes in each corner. Machine-stitch the buttonholes and cut the centres.

10 Sew buttons on to the corners of the hessian pillow cover, and button the voile cover over the top.

Right: This all-white scheme is practical as well as beautiful — the voile covers are simply unbuttoned from the main covers when they require cleaning.

PURE PLASTIC

A plastic tablecloth is invaluable on a table that gets a lot of use, as it can be wiped clean in seconds. To make it attractive as well as practical, why not cut a shaped trim and make a design along the edge using a hole punch?

2 Cut the edging shape with sharp dressmaker's scissors.

1 Measure your table and cut the plastic fabric to the required size. Draw up and cut out a cardboard template or trace the template from the back of the book for the scalloped edge. Draw around the template on the wrong side of the plastic fabric.

3 Punch out a design with a hole punch. You could thread ribbon, string or rope through the holes, to add even more interest.

TACTILE TABLECLOTH

A mass of trimmings is now available and a trip around the haberdashery department will, with a little imagination, generate any number of ideas. Here, simple upholsterer's webbing was used to edge a hessian cloth. The webbing was decorated with string in very loose loops.

1 Cut the hessian to the size of the tablecloth you require, allowing for hems. Turn under the hems and pin, tack, press and machine-stitch. Cut a length of webbing to go round all four sides. Pin and machine-stitch the webbing around the edge.

YOU WILL NEED

- ◆ about 2m/2yd hessian
- ◆ dressmaker's scissors
- ◆ dressmaker's pins
- ◆ needle and tacking thread
- ◆ iron
- ◆ sewing machine
- ◆ matching sewing thread
- ◆ 8m/8¾ yd webbing
- ◆ brown string

2 Lay the string on the webbing and twist to experiment with different designs.

3 Pin, tack and hand-stitch the string to the webbing, to hold it securely. It doesn't matter if there are gaps in the stitching; the looseness of the string is all part of the effect.

ON THE SHELF

Everyone has shelves somewhere about the home but how many of us have thought of dressing them with different styles of edging? This project includes three different designs using natural materials that would be suitable for a kitchen. Many other ideas, such as colourful fabrics, scalloped edging, ribbons, shells, buttons and bows, would be much better suited to bedrooms and bathrooms. Experiment with anything and everything around the home and you'll be surprised at just how innovative and exciting shelf edging can be. If you fix your trimmings with double-sided tape, they can be removed in an instant so you can change the designs as often as you like.

YOU WILL NEED

- ◆ tape measure
- ◆ string
- ◆ scissors
- ◆ sticky tape
- ◆ red raffia
- ◆ Chinese-language newspaper
- ◆ pencil
- ◆ double-sided tape or drawing pins

1 Measure the length of your shelf.

2 Cut a piece of string about 5cm/2in longer than the shelf, so it can turn around the corners.

3 Cut more lengths of string, approximately 15–20cm/6–8in long.

4 Gather together bunches of about three lengths of string.

5 Fold the bunches into loops and then pass the ends over the string and through the centre of the loop. Pull the loops taut to secure them. You can tape the string to the work surface if it makes it easier to work on it.

6 Cut small pieces of red raffia and tie them into small knots between every two or three strands of looped string. Cut the raffia close to the knot.

7 For the newspaper edging, measure the shelf. Cut strips the length of the shelf, and the depth you require. Fold each strip, concertina-fashion.

8 Experiment by drawing different designs on to each folded strip.

9 Cut out the edging shapes. Open them out and smooth them flat.

10 For the raffia edging, cut a piece of raffia the length of the shelf. Cut many short lengths of raffia.

12 Tighten the loops, and fill in any gaps with more loops.

14 Use double-sided tape or drawing pins to attach the trimmings to the edge of each shelf.

11 Using one strand at a time, loop them on to the main piece, as for the string edging.

13 Trim all the ends to one length to make an even fringe.

Opposite: Shelf edging gives scope for tremendous creativity. Here, home-made fringes of raffia and string and a decorative edge cut from a Chinese-language newspaper soften wooden kitchen shelves.

IN THE ROUND

Choose the primary colours of blue and red and team them with white for a crisp, clean look with a slightly nautical feel. Felt is a lovely way to trim plain fabrics, whether on shoe bags, linen bags, throws or cushions.

1 Find a round template: it could be a tin lid, coin or anything similar. Place the template on the felt, and draw round the template with a fabric marker. Cut around the circle with pinking shears.

YOU WILL NEED

- ◆ round template
- ◆ 2 squares of red felt, about 20 x 20cm / 8 x 8in
- ◆ 2 squares of blue felt, about 20 x 20cm / 8 x 8in
- ◆ dressmaker's pins
- ◆ fabric marker
- ◆ pinking shears
- ◆ blue cord
- ◆ string
- ◆ needle and matching sewing thread
- ◆ fabric item such as a shoebag or quilt

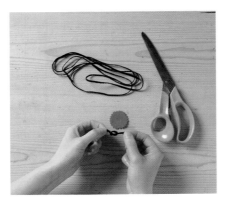

2 Pin two circles together, knot short lengths of cord and sew them on to the circles.

3 Repeat with lengths of string. Sew the circles on to your shoe bag, quilt or other items.

DRESSING FOR DINNER

For very special occasions, why not take a tip from etiquette books, and give it a new twist, by preparing corsages for your chairs? Choose a style of dressing suited to the style of your furniture. Simple country chairs call for understated trimmings, whereas a fancy French one requires something much more ornate.

YOU WILL NEED

♦ silk or fresh flowers
♦ fresh greenery
♦ florist's wire
♦ scissors
♦ 2m/2yd organza ribbon

1 Gather together your flowers and greenery. Using florist's wire, begin to wire together the stems. Using silk flowers makes life easier, because they bend to whatever shape you require.

2 Continue binding in flowers and greenery, to make an attractive corsage. Trim the stems and tuck in any ends.

3 When you're satisfied with the shape, finish with a ribbon bow. Make a wire hook to fix the corsage to the chair. If you like, make an arrangement that can be taken from the chair and worn or taken home at the end of the evening.

PRETTY POTS

Miniature topiary looks charming on a windowsill, but don't forget to make the most of their containers. Terracotta pots can be treated to a variety of embellishments, from tassels to tape.

YOU WILL NEED

- ◆ florist's dry foam block
- ◆ sharp knife
- ◆ 3 old terracotta pots
- ◆ 2 straight twigs
- ◆ glue gun and glue sticks
- ◆ 2 florist's dry foam balls
- ◆ fresh foliage such as box or privet
- ◆ selection of pebbles
- ◆ curtain weight
- ◆ fine string
- ◆ string tassels
- ◆ masking tape
- ◆ craft knife
- ◆ self-healing cutting mat
- ◆ matt varnish
- ◆ paintbrush

1 Cut the foam blocks in half and cut each block to fit into the pots. Position the foam in the pots. Insert the twigs and glue them in place, to act as the stems of the trees. Glue the foam balls on top.

3 Cover the foam in the pots with a layer of small pebbles.

2 Cut small pieces of foliage and insert them in the balls, to give a casual, carefree effect.

4 Thread the curtain weight on to string and tie it around one of the pots. Decorate the other pots with tassels, or designs cut from masking tape with a craft knife. Varnish to make the masking tape secure.

MATERIALS

You can use just about any material that catches your eye for trimmings. Although haberdashers and specialist soft furnishing shops were always the traditional suppliers of trimmings such as tassels and ribbons, look beyond the expected sources for rich pickings. For natural materials in neutral colours, you could visit yachting chandlers for lengths of rope in different thicknesses and textures. Try garden centres for twine and raffia and art supply shops for canvas and hessian. Take a detour from the high street and comb the beach for interesting shells, driftwood and pebbles.

If you are looking for glamour and sparkle, bead shops have a wonderful array of diamanté, artificial "jewels" and plastic bone to dress up glasses, napkins, table tops and boxes.

Ribbons play such a big part in trimming, that it is worth searching out the most unusual ones possible.

Closer to home, your local post office will supply humble items such as parcel string, corrugated cardboard and plain brown parcel paper – which

sound unappealing but can be used to embellish anything from boxes to bedheads.

The only rule to using materials for trimming is to open your eyes, collect what appeals to you and let your imagination take over.

Right: Trimming materials might include natural materials such as stones, leaves and dried materials (1); textured fabrics such as hessian (2); tassels made of cord, ribbon or raffia (3); organza ribbon (4); strings of beads or necklaces (5); shells and starfish (6); fabric paint (7); apple twigs (8); loose beads (9); string (10); and corrugated cardboard (11).

TECHNIQUES

Embellishing is all about gluing, sticking, tying, or sewing — basically adding to existing objects, to make the simple, sensational. Part of the joy of decorating in this way is that there are no specific, professional techniques to learn, just some handy shortcuts that will make the job easier. Some quick and easy fixing techniques have been suggested here. Tassels will add glamour to any object, and although there are specialist shops available, they can be made at home using the materials of your choice — from silk embroidery thread to fine wire. Even the most basic of embroidery stitches will perk up plain fabric items such as napkins or pillowcases. You may not feel you have the expertise to produce intricate hand embroidery, but use thick threads in bold colours to produce large, eye-catching stitches to make your own style statement.

Blanket stitch

Fasten the working thread securely just under the fabric edge, then insert the needle down into the fabric, at the desired distance from the edge. The needle should always be at right angles to the edge, or the stitches will become uneven. Hold the working thread under the needle, and pull the point of the needle through.

Buttonhole stitch

Back stitch

Bring the needle and thread up to the top side of the fabric. Re-insert the needle about 3mm/⅛in behnd the point where the thread came out. Now bring the needle back up to the top, 3mm/⅛in to the front of the first point. Continue in this way, to produce what appears to be one continuous line of stitches.

This stitch is worked in the opposite direction to blanket stitch. Insert the needle upwards through the fabric, at the desired distance from the edge. Twist the working thread around the point of the needle. Pull the needle through the fabric, bringing the knot that has formed to the raw edge.

Using a glue gun

Hot glue will allow you to take short-cuts to fixing objects. Here, short ends of wire were glued to shells, to allow them to be tied to curtain rails, or twisted on to lengths of muslin. Always follow the manufacturer's instructions for your particular model of glue gun. Once the gun has heated sufficiently the glue becomes liquid – take great care as it will burn if in contact with the skin. Place a small dot of glue on the surface of the object, then hold the wire on the hot glue for a few seconds to allow it to set completely.

Drilling holes

An alternative way of fixing objects like shells or driftwood is to drill a small hole into each, then thread a length of wire, raffia or string through the hole. For this you will need the finest drill bit available. To keep the drill from sliding off the surface, place a piece of masking tape over the spot you wish to drill, then bore the hole. Remove the masking tape and thread your chosen material through the drilled hole.

Positioning and fixing eyelets

Eyelet holes are an effective way of adding impact to plain fabrics for curtains or even bed covers. If you are using a fairly fine fabric, you may wish to add extra body by adding interfacing to the hem. Iron-on interfacing is very easy to use. Cut the interfacing to half the depth of the hem, minus the seam allowance, and iron in place. Next mark the positions of the eyelets at equal distances along the top of the curtain. Follow the manufacturer's instructions for punching the hole in the fabric, then place the eyelets in position and hammer to secure. Remember to work on a very solid surface – one hard blow with the hammer should secure each eyelet.

Making tassels

1 Take 3–4 long strands of raffia. Hold together firmly, then wind them back and forth in a lazy S-shape to form a skein.

3 Use another piece of raffia to bind tightly round the centre of the skein. Tie in a firm knot (this is the centre point of the tassel), leaving two long ends that will later form the tie of the tassle. Fold the skein in half, where it has been secured, then wrap another length of raffia around this, approximately 3mm/⅛in from the top, to form the tassel shape. Trim the looped ends to all the same length.

4 Split the two centre raffia lengths to form three (raffia splits very easily). Plait to form a neat tie for the tassel, then knot when the correct length is achieved.

2 Trim off the ragged excess on the ends of the raffia.

5 To add more body to the tassel, take a dressmaker's pin or needle and run it down each raffia strand two or three times. This will split each strand of raffia and make the tassel more full.

TEMPLATES

A A B B B C C
D D E E F F F
G G G H H H I I
I I K K L L L
M M M N N O

scalloped edge

ACKNOWLEDGEMENTS

The author and publishers would like to thank the following for the loan of materials for photography:

Damask Furnishings and Finery
3-4 Broxholme House
New Kings Road
London SW6
(fine voile napkins, p28)

Harley Antiques
295 Lillie Road
London SW6
(table, p21; map box, pp38–9)

The Hop Shop
Castle Farm
Shoreham
Sevenoaks, Kent
TN1 4B
(Jacket: dried leaves on lampshade)

Josephine Ryan Antiques
335 Lillie Road
London SW6
(glass bottles without stoppers, p28; armchair, painter's desk, folding table, plaster shapes, white jug, candlestick, clock face and wooden horse, p65)

299 Antiques
299 Lillie Road
London SW6
(chair, p45; chair, pp72–3)

The author would like to thank Charles Shirvell for all his help and creative input, and Josh George for his assistance in the studio.

INDEX